In Case I Die
A Planning Guide

By Jon Jaques, CPA

In Case I Die
A Planning Guide

Copyright © 2011
Skylo, Inc.
All Rights Reserved

The author can be reached at:

Jon Jaques, CPA
Skylo, Inc.
752 S Church Street
Murfreesboro, TN 37130
jon@skyloinc.com
www.skyloinc.com

WARNING

This digital book is a copyrighted product of Skylo, Inc. All rights are reserved under law. No unauthorized duplication of any kind is allowed. Any unauthorized duplication will be prosecuted to the full extent of the law.

This digital book is provided for private, individual use only, and cannot be used in any other setting without prior written approval and/or license.

If you did not receive this from the website www.skyloinc.com, please send a PayPal payment of $9.95 to the email address sales@skyloinc.com

Table of Contents

4	Dedication
5	Forward
6	About Jon Jaques
7	Demographic Information
8	Last Will & Testament
9	Power of Attorney
10	Medical Directive
11	Trust Paperwork
12	Guardianship of Minors Paperwork
13	Location of Other Important Documents
14	Obituary Comments
15	Funeral Service Comments
16	Headstone & Grave Marker Comments
17	Provisions for Veterans Location of Form DD-214
18	Memberships in Organizations
19	Special Friends to Contact
20	Organizations to Contact
21	Religious Contacts
22	Family Contacts
23	Online Account Passwords
24	Bank Accounts, Banks and Safe Deposit Boxes
25	Investment Accounts
26	Online Accounts
27	Copies of Past Three Years Tax Returns and Supporting Documents
28	Summary of Life Insurance and Companies
29	Location of Life Insurance Policies
30	Summary of Retirement Plans
31	Annuities and Other Deferred Payments
32	Summary of Real Estate Owned
33	Other Assets to Consider
34	Business Assets Owned
35	Special Notes about Business Assets
36	Special Collections Owned (Coins, Guns, etc.)
37	Notes on Disposition of Special Collections
38	Special Sentimental Items
39	Key People - Attorney
40	Key People - Life Insurance Agents
41	Key People - Accountant/Tax Preparer
42	Key People - Executor/Co-Executor/Sub. Executor
43	Key People - Banker
44	Key People - Investment Advisor
45	Major Debts/Creditors/Mortgages
46	Assets & Debts Owned Jointly
47	Notes to Spouse
48-50	Notes to Children
51	Life Accomplishments
52	Special Instructons (Outside of Will)

In Case I Die
A Planning Guide

Dedication

To my brother, Bob Jaques, Jr.,
who showed great courage
in the face of health issues
that would have easily defeated
a lesser person.

Smooth sailing, fair winds, and God's speed.

DISCLOSURE

This planning guide does not replace your properly prepared and executed last will and testament. You should consult appropriate legal guidance for the proper preparation of your will, medical directives, trust documents, and other documents.
You should also consult the appropriate professional advice of other professionals for tax and accounting advice.

The publisher does not provide legal, accounting, tax, or other professional guidance.

Forward

Breaking news! We are headed to meet our Maker; it's just a matter of when.

As a certified public accountant, I have met with many families over the past twenty years dealing with the loss of a loved one. Some families are able to deal with the many details of a death -- others are thrown into total chaos. I have seen family fights, sibling/parent divisions, unlocated or unknown assets, unretrievable digital records, wrong beneficiaries, and other issues.

Sadly, many of these headaches and heartaches could have been avoided. Simple planning, such as this guide, would have gone a long way in preventing most the road bumps and hurt feelings.

"Those who fail to plan, plan to fail," is a saying we have all heard. This has never been truer than planning your affairs in case you die! More than half of all deaths come unexpectedly! Car accidents, sudden heart attack or stroke, victim of violence, or unforeseen accident have all claimed clients of mine in the past two years. Sadly, NONE were prepared for their sudden death!

Completing this planning guide will help your loved ones handle your affairs. This guide should be reviewed and updated on each birthday. Copies should be provided to your trusted advisors and the original kept sealed in a safe place that your next-of-kin can easily access.

Word of caution – I would not suggest keeping the original in a safe deposit box due to some states requiring an inventory before contents are released. Many of the provisions of your planning guide are time sensitive and an inventory delay would be impractical.

About Jon Jaques, CPA

Jon Jaques has been a certified public accountant (CPA) since 1990. This guide is the result of working with many families, businesses, and other organizations who have dealt with sudden death. Since 1991, Jon has operated his own accounting firm, specializing in small businesses, complex family planning, and services to the not-for-profit community. Also licensed as a financial services and insurance professional, Jon has worked with many families to help plan for successful retirement and orderly disposition of assets to subsequent generations.

Jon is actively involved in Boy Scouts, his church, and the United States Submarine Veterans organization.

Along with his wife, Karen, Jon has two wonderful children, Sky and Lo. The Jaques' make their home in Murfreesboro, Tennessee.

Demographic Information

Name: _____

Address: _____

City & State: _____

Date of birth: _____

Place of birth: _____

Father's name: _____

Mother's name: _____

COPIES OF THIS PLANNING GUIDE WERE GIVEN TO:

1. _____

2. _____

3. _____

Last Will & Testament

Locations:_____

Who has copies? _____

_____

_____

Signed and witnessed? _____

Key Provisions:

- _____

- _____

- _____

- _____

- _____

Power of Attorney

Locations: _____

Who has copies? _____

_____

_____

Key Provisions:

- _____

- _____

- _____

- _____

- _____

Medical Directive

Locations:_____

Who has copies? _____

_____

_____

Key Provisions:

- _____

- _____

- _____

- _____

- _____

Trust Paperwork

Locations:_____

Who has copies? _____

_____

_____

Key Provisions:

- _____

- _____

- _____

- _____

- _____

Guardianship of Minors Paperwork

Locations:_____

Who has copies? _____

_____

_____

Key Provisions:

- _____

- _____

- _____

- _____

- _____

Location of Other Important Documents

Marriage Certificate: _____

Divorce Papers: _____

Property Deeds: _____

Promissory Notes Receivable: _____

Other:

- _____

- _____

- _____

- _____

- _____

Obituary Comments

Funeral Service Comments

Headstone & Grave Marker Comments

Provisions for Veterans Location of Form DD-214

Locations: _____

Who has copies? _____

_____

_____

Key Provisions:

- _____

- _____

- _____

- _____

- _____

Eligible for Military Headstone or Footstone? _____

Please Contact Veteran's Administration: _____

Memberships in Organizations

1. _____

2. _____

3. _____

4. _____

5. _____

6. _____

7. _____

8. _____

9. _____

10. _____

Special Friends to Contact

SAME DAY:

1. _____
2. _____
3. _____
4. _____
5. _____
6. _____

NEXT DAY:

1. _____
2. _____
3. _____
4. _____
5. _____
6. _____

NEXT MONTH:

1. _____
2. _____
3. _____
4. _____
5. _____
6. _____

OTHER:

1. _____
   _____
2. _____
   _____
3. _____
   _____
4. _____
   _____
5. _____
   _____
6. _____
   _____
7. _____
   _____

Organizations to Contact

SAME DAY:

1. _____
2. _____
3. _____
4. _____
5. _____
6. _____

NEXT DAY:

1. _____
2. _____
3. _____
4. _____
5. _____
6. _____

NEXT MONTH:

1. _____
2. _____
3. _____
4. _____
5. _____
6. _____

NOTES:

1. _____
   _____
2. _____
   _____
3. _____
   _____
4. _____
   _____
5. _____
   _____
6. _____
   _____
7. _____
   _____

Religious Contacts

SAME DAY:

1. _____
2. _____
3. _____
4. _____
5. _____
6. _____

NEXT DAY:

1. _____
2. _____
3. _____
4. _____
5. _____
6. _____

NEXT MONTH:

1. _____
2. _____
3. _____
4. _____
5. _____
6. _____

NOTES:

1. _____
   _____
2. _____
   _____
3. _____
   _____
4. _____
   _____
5. _____
   _____
6. _____
   _____
7. _____
   _____

Family Contacts

SAME DAY:

1. _____
2. _____
3. _____
4. _____
5. _____
6. _____

NEXT DAY:

1. _____
2. _____
3. _____
4. _____
5. _____
6. _____

NEXT MONTH:

1. _____
2. _____
3. _____
4. _____
5. _____
6. _____

NOTES:

1. _____
   _____
2. _____
   _____
3. _____
   _____
4. _____
   _____
5. _____
   _____
6. _____
   _____
7. _____
   _____

Online Account Passwords

- For what? _____
- Password: _____
- Location: _____

- For what? _____
- Password: _____
- Location: _____

- For what? _____
- Password: _____
- Location: _____

- For what? _____
- Password: _____
- Location: _____

- For what? _____
- Password: _____
- Location: _____

In Case I Die
A Planning Guide

Bank Accounts, Banks, and Safe Deposit Boxes

Bank: _____

Accounts: _____

Bank: _____

Accounts: _____

Safe Deposit Box Location: _____

Who has key? _____

Authorized openers: _____

Other Notes: _____

_____

_____

_____

_____

In Case I Die
A Planning Guide

Investment Accounts

1. Broker: _____

Acct. Number: _____

2. Broker: _____

Acct. Number: _____

3. Broker: _____

Acct. Number: _____

4. Broker: _____

Acct. Number: _____

5. Broker: _____

Acct. Number: _____

Online Accounts

1. Bank: _____

Acct. Number: _____

2. Bank: _____

Acct. Number: _____

3. Bank: _____

Acct. Number: _____

4. Other: _____

Acct. Number: _____

5. Other: _____

Acct. Number: _____

Copies of Past Three Years Tax Returns and Supporting Documents

Locations:_____

Who has copies? _____

_____

_____

Key Provisions:

- _____

- _____

- _____

- _____

- _____

Summary of Life Insurance and Companies

Company:_____

Amount:_____

Beneficiary:_____

Agent: _____

Other Notes: _____

_____

_____

_____

_____

_____

Note: You can print multiple copies of this page to accommodate additional insurance policies.

Location of Life Insurance Policies

Locations:_____

Who has copies? _____

_____

_____

Key Provisions:

- _____

- _____

- _____

- _____

- _____

Note: You can print multiple copies of this page to accommodate additional insurance policies.

Summary of Retirement Plans

1. Type: _____ Beneficiary: _____

   Custodian: _____ Acct. Number: _____

2. Type: _____ Beneficiary: _____

   Custodian: _____ Acct. Number: _____

3. Type: _____ Beneficiary: _____

   Custodian: _____ Acct. Number: _____

4. Type: _____ Beneficiary: _____

   Custodian: _____ Acct. Number: _____

5. Type: _____ Beneficiary: _____

   Custodian: _____ Acct. Number: _____

Annuities and Other Deferred Payments

1. Type: _____   Beneficiary: _____

   Company: _____   Acct. Number: _____

2. Type: _____   Beneficiary: _____

   Company: _____   Acct. Number: _____

3. Type: _____   Beneficiary: _____

   Company: _____   Acct. Number: _____

4. Type: _____   Beneficiary: _____

   Company: _____   Acct. Number: _____

5. Type: _____   Beneficiary: _____

   Company: _____   Acct. Number: _____

Summary of Real Estate Owned

1. Address: _____

   Type: _____ Ownership: _____

2. Address: _____

   Type: _____ Ownership: _____

3. Address: _____

   Type: _____ Ownership: _____

4. Address: _____

   Type: _____ Ownership: _____

5. Address: _____

   Type: _____ Ownership: _____

Other Assets to Consider

1. _____

2. _____

3. _____

4. _____

5. _____

6. _____

7. _____

8. _____

In Case I Die
A Planning Guide

Business Assets Owned

1. _____

2. _____

3. _____

4. _____

5. _____

6. _____

7. _____

8. _____

In Case I Die
A Planning Guide

Special Notes about Business Assets

Special Collections Owned
(Coins, Guns, ect.)

- _____
- _____
- _____
- _____
- _____
- _____
- _____
- _____
- _____
- _____
- _____
- _____

Notes on Disposition of Special Collections

Special Sentimental Items

- _____
- _____
- _____
- _____
- _____
- _____
- _____
- _____
- _____
- _____
- _____
- _____

Key People - Attorney

Name: _____

Address: _____

_____

_____

Phone:

_____

_____

_____

E-mail:

_____

_____

When to notify: _____

Key People - Life Insurance Agents

Name:_____

Address: _____

_____

_____

Phone:

_____

_____

_____

E-mail:

_____

_____

When to notify: _____

Key People - Accountant/Tax Preparer

Name: _____

Address: _____

_____

_____

Phone:

_____

_____

E-mail:

_____

_____

When to notify: _____

Key People - Executor/Co-Executor/Sub. Executor

Name: _____

Address: _____

    _____

    _____

Phone:

_____

_____

_____

E-mail:

_____

_____

When to notify: _____

Key People - Banker

Name: _____

Address: _____

_____

_____

Phone:

_____

_____

_____

E-mail:

_____

_____

When to notify: _____

Key People - Investment Advisor

Name: _____

Address: _____

_____

_____

Phone:

_____

_____

E-mail:

_____

_____

When to notify: _____

Major Debts/Creditors/Mortgages

1. _____

2. _____

3. _____

4. _____

5. _____

6. _____

Notes:

In Case I Die
A Planning Guide

Assets & Debts Owned Jointly

1. _____

2. _____

3. _____

4. _____

5. _____

6. _____

Notes:

Notes to Spouse

Notes to Child (1)

Notes to Child (2)

Notes to Child (3)

Life Accomplishments

1. _____

2. _____

3. _____

4. _____

5. _____

6. _____

7. _____

8. _____

9. _____

10. _____

Special Instructions (Outside of Will)

In Case I Die
A Planning Guide

Copyright © 2011
Skylo, Inc.
All Rights Reserved

The author can be reached at:

Jon Jaques, CPA
Skylo, Inc.
752 S Church Street • Murfreesboro, TN 37130
jon@skyloinc.com • www.skyloinc.com

Book Design by Rick Johnson
rickjohnsongraphics@gmail.com